SARAH HATTON KNITS 10 SIMPLE CROCHET
PROJECTS FOR COSY HOMES

First published in Great Britain in 2016 by
Quail Publishing Limited
www.quailpublishing.co.uk

Copyright © Quail Publishing 2016

Designs: Sarah Hatton
Photography: India Hobson
Styling: Sarah Hatton & India Hobson
Graphic Design: Quail Studio

ISBN: 978-0-9927707-4-7

Printed in the United Kingdom

SARAH HATTON KNITS

10 SIMPLE

CROCHET PROJECTS FOR COSY HOMES

Q

QUAIL

Rope Necklaces by Peggypeg see credits pg.46

SLOUCHY SWEATER

page. 14

Pot by Grey Suit Clay
Tea towel and wooden spoon by Roanna Wellls
see credits pg.46

POTS & DOILY

page. 18 & 37

TABLE RUNNER

page. 22

DOILY BUNTING

page. 37

SIMPLE SHOPPING BAG

page. 26

Small Pot by Grey Suit Clay, Lino Cut Print by James Green see credits pg.46

CROCHET DOTS NECKLACE

page. 28

GRANNY SQUARE
CUSHION & BLANKET

page. 30 & 34

Picture by Roanna Wells see credits pg.46

ENVELOPE CUSHION

page. 39

SHELL STITCH
BED RUNNER

page. 42

SLOUCHY SWEATER
rowan creative focus worsted

Materials List

YARN
Rowan Creative Focus Worsted
6 [7:7:8:9] x 100gm
(shown in Nickel 00401)

HOOK
6mm (UK 4/US J10) crochet hook

TO FIT BUST

S	M	L	XL	XXL
81-86	91-96	102-107	112-117	122-127cm
32-34	36-38	40-42	44-46	48-50 in

ACTUAL WIDTH (LAID FLAT)

50	55	62	69	76 cm
19¾	21½	24/2	27	30 in

LENGTH

56	58	60	62	64 cm
22	22¾	23½	24½	25¼ in

SLEEVE LENGTH (PLUS TURNBACK)

32	33	34	34	34 cm
12½	13	13¼	13¼	13¼ in

TENSION

17 stitches and 9 rows measures 10cm/4in over body pattern using 6mm (US J10) crochet hook.

US crocheters please see page 44 for information about the UK/US terminology conversion.

Make 73 [82:89:96:102] chains.

Foundation row : Work 1 double crochet into 2nd chain from hook, work 1 double crochet into each stitch to end, turn.
72 [81:88:95:101] stitches.

Row 1: Chain 3, miss 1 stitch, 1 treble into each stitch to end, work 1 treble into chain at beginning of last row.

Row 2: 1 chain, miss 1 stitch, 1 double crochet into each stitch to end, work 1 double crochet into 3rd chain at beginning of last row.

Repeat row 1 once more.

Next row: 1 chain, miss 1 stitch, 1 double crochet into next 2 [6:4:1:6] stitches, (2 double crochet into next stitch, 1 double crochet into next 4 [4:4:5:5] stitches) 13 [13:15:15:17] times, 2 double crochet into next stitch, 1 double crochet into each stitch to end, work 1 double crochet into 3rd chain at beginning of last row. 85 [94:103:112:118] stitches.

Main pattern foundation row: Chain 3, 1 treble into next stitch, * skip 1 stitch, 1 treble into next stitch, 1 chain, 1 treble into next st, repeat from * to last 2 stitches, skip 1 stitch, work 1 treble into chain at beginning of last row, turn.

Row 1: Chain 3, miss 1 treble, * work (1 treble, 1 chain, 1 treble) into next chain space, miss next 2 trebles, repeat from * to end, work 1 treble into 3rd chain at beginning of last row, turn.

Row 1 sets pattern and is repeated throughout.

Continue in pattern until work measures 56 [58:60:62:64]cm/22 [22¾:23½:24½:25¼]in.

Fasten off.

FRONT
Work as given for Back until Front measures 53 [55:57:59:61]cm/21 [21½:22½:23¼:24]in. (You should have worked 2 pattern repeats less than the back).

Shape front neck

Next row: Chain 3, miss 1 treble, work (1 treble, 1 chain, 1 treble) into 8 [9:10:11:12] next chain spaces, work 1 treble into next treble, turn.

Next row: Chain 3, miss 1 treble,* work (1 treble, 1 chain, 1 treble) into next chain space, miss next 2 trebles, repeat from * to end, work 1 treble into 3rd chain at beginning of last row. Fasten off.

Leave 12 [13:14:15:16] chain spaces at centre of body unworked, rejoin yarn to next treble,

Next row: Chain 3, miss 1 treble, work (1 treble, 1 chain, 1 treble) into 8 [9:10:11:12] next chain spaces, work 1 treble into next treble, turn.

Next row: Chain 3, miss 1 treble, * work (1 treble, 1 chain, 1 treble) into next chain space, miss 2 trebles, repeat from * to end, work 1 treble into 3rd chain at beginning of last row. Fasten off.

SLEEVES (Both alike)
Make 45 [46:48:49:51] chains.

Foundation row : Work 1 double crochet into 2nd chain from hook, work 1 double crochet into each stitch to end, turn.

44 [45:47:48:50] stitches.

Row 1: Chain 3, miss 1 treble, 1 treble into each stitch to end, work 1 treble into chain at beginning of last row.

Row 2: 1 chain, miss 1 treble, 1 double crochet into each stitch to end, work 1 double crochet into 3rd chain at beginning of last row.

These 2 rows set pattern.

Work 3 rows more as set.

Place a marker at each end of next row to denote turnback.

Work 5 rows more.

Increase 1 stitch by working into 1 stitch twice at each end of row on next and 1 [3:3:5:5] following alternate rows, then on 6 [5:5:4:4] following 3rd rows.
60 [63:65:68:70] stitches.

Continue without shaping until sleeve measures 32 [33:34:34:34] cm/12½ [13:13¼:13¼:13¼]in from markers.

Shape sleeve top

Next row: Slip stitch across first 6 stitches, 1 chain, 1 double crochet into each stitch to last 6 stitches, turn.

Repeat this row 4 times more.

Fasten off.

MAKING UP
Join both shoulder seams.

With RS facing, rejoin yarn to left side of front neck, work 6 double crochet down side of front neck, 24 [26:28:30:32] double crochet from front neck, 6 double crochet up right side of front neck and 24 [26:28:30:32] double crochet from back neck, slip stitch to first stitch to join. 60 [64:68:72:74] stitches.

Round 1: 3 chain, 1 treble into each stitch to end, slip stitch to 3rd chain at beginning of round to join.

Round 2: 1 chain, * 1 double crochet into each stitch to end, slip stitch to first chain to join.

Repeat these 2 rounds twice more. Fasten off.

Place markers 22 [23:24:25:26] cm/8½ [9:9½:10:10¼]in down from shoulder. Sew sleeves in place between these markers. Join side and sleeve seams.

POTS
rowan handknit cotton

Materials List

YARN
Rowan Handknit Cotton
Large - 2 x 50gm
Medium - 2 x 50gm
Small - 1 x 50gm
Shown in Slate 347 (A)
Plus oddments of contrast yarn (B)
shown in Bleached 263.

HOOK
3.5mm (UK 9/US E4) crochet
hook or size required to achieve
correct tension.

SIZES

Large – Approx 19cm (7½in) wide and 10cm (4in) deep

Medium – Approx 17cm (6¾in) wide and 15cm (6in) deep

Small – Approx 9cm (3½in) wide and 8cm (3¼in) deep

TENSION

18 stitches and 18 rows to 10cm (4in) measured over pattern on 3.5mm hook.

US crocheters please see page 44 for information about the UK/US terminology conversion.

LARGE POT
Base section

Using A make 4 chains, slip stitch into 1st chain to form a ring.

Round 1: 1 chain, 9 double crochet into ring, slip stitch to first chain to join.

Round 2: 1 chain, 2 double crochet into each stitch, slip stitch to first chain to join. 18 stitches.

Round 3: 1 chain, 1 double crochet into each stitch, slip stitch to first chain to join.

Round 4: 1 chain, * 2 double crochet into next stitch, 1 double crochet into next stitch, repeat from * to end, slip stitch to first chain to join. 27 stitches.

Round 5: 1 chain, * 2 double crochet into next stitch, 1 double crochet into next 2 stitches, repeat from * to end, slip stitch to first chain to join. 36 stitches.

Round 6: Work as round 3.

Round 7: 1 chain, * 2 double crochet into next stitch, 1 double crochet into next 3 stitches, repeat from * to end, slip stitch to first chain to join. 45 stitches.

Round 8: 1 chain, * 2 double crochet into next stitch, 1 double crochet into next 4 stitches, repeat from * to end, slip stitch to first chain to join. 54 stitches.

Round 9: Work as round 3.

Round 10: 1 chain, * 2 double crochet into next stitch, 1 double crochet into next 5 stitches, repeat from * to end, slip stitch to first chain to join. 63 stitches.

Round 11: 1 chain, * 2 double crochet into next stitch, 1 double crochet into next 6 stitches, repeat from * to end, slip stitch to first chain to join. 72 stitches.

Round 12: Work as round 3.

Round 13: 1 chain, * 2 double crochet into next stitch, 1 double crochet into next 7 stitches, repeat from * to end, slip stitch to first chain to join. 81 stitches.

Round 14: 1 chain, * 2 double crochet into next stitch, 1 double crochet into next 8 stitches, repeat from * to end, slip stitch to first chain to join. 90 stitches.

Round 15: Work as round 3.

Round 16: 1 chain, * 2 double crochet into next stitch, 1 double crochet into next 9 stitches, repeat from * to end, slip stitch to first chain to join. 99 stitches.

Round 17: 1 chain, * 2 double crochet into next stitch, 1 double crochet into next 10 stitches, repeat from * to end, slip stitch to first chain to join. 108 stitches.

Round 18: Work as round 3.

Round 19: 1 chain, * 2 double crochet into next stitch, 1 double crochet into next 11 stitches, repeat from * to end, slip stitch to first chain to join. 117 stitches.

Round 20: 1 chain, * 2 double crochet into next stitch, 1 double crochet into next 12 stitches, repeat from * to end, slip stitch to first chain to join. 126 stitches.

Side section

Round 1: 1 chain, 1 double crochet into each stitch to end, slip stitch to first chain to join.

Round 2: 2 chain, 1 half treble into each stitch to end, slip stitch to 2nd chain at beginning of round to join.

Rep these 2 rounds until work measures 8cm/3¼in, ending with row 1.

Next round: Work as given for round 2 but decrease 2 stitches (by working two stitches together) at end of round. 124 stitches.

You will now need to turn you work in order for the bobble to form correctly.

Bobble round : Using B, 1 chain, * 1 double crochet into next 3 stitches, treble 3 together into next stitch, repeat from * to end, slip stitch to chain at beg of round to join, turn work so right side is facing.

Using A, beginning with round 2, work 3 rounds more. Fasten off.

MEDIUM POT
Work as set for large pot to round 16.

Side section

Round 1: 1 chain, 1 double crochet into each stitch to end, slip stitch to first chain to join.

Round 2: 1 chain, 1 half treble into each stitch to end, slip stitch to first chain to join.

Rep these 2 rounds until work measures 9cm/3½in ending with round 1.

Next round: Work as given for round 2 but increase 1 stitch by working into 1 stitch twice. 100 stitches. You will now need to turn you work in order for the bobble to form correctly.

Bobble round : Using B, 1 chain, * 1 double crochet into next 3 stitches, treble 3 together into next stitch, repeat from * to end, slip stitch to chain at beginning of round to join, turn work show right side is facing.

Using A, beginning with round 2, work 3 rounds.

Next round:-Using B, work as round 1.

Next round: Using A, work as round 2.

Repeat these 2 rounds once more.

Next round:-Using B, work as round 1. Fasten off.

SMALL POT
Work as set for large pot to round 8.

Side section

Round 1: 1 chain, 1 double crochet into each stitch to end, slip stitch to first chain to join.

Round 2: 1 chain, 1 half treble into each stitch to end, slip stitch to first chain to join.

Rep these 2 rounds once more.

Bobble round : Using B, 1 chain, 1 double crochet into next 3 stitches,

treble 3 together into next stitch, repeat from * to end, slip stitch to chain at beg of round to join, turn work so right side is facing.

Using A, beginning with round 2, continue in pattern as set until work measures 8cm/3¼in. Fasten off.

You can easily alter the shape of these pots by increasing the base as set until it reaches the size required, then working the sides as set. The bobble row requires a multiple of 4 stitches so you may need to alter the number of stitches you have on the round before.

TABLE RUNNER
rowan handknit cotton

Materials List

YARN
Rowan Handknit Cotton
Our version took 3 x 50gm with
yarn to spare.
We used Bleached 263 and made
10 daisy, 6 star, 8 spoked and 9
cartwheel motifs.

HOOK
4mm (UK8/USG6) crochet hook or size
required to achieve correct tension.

TENSION

Trebles should be 1.5cm in height worked on 5mm hook.

US crocheters please see page 44 for information about the UK/US terminology conversion.

DAISY

Make 5 chains and slip stitch into 1st chain to form a ring.

Round 1: 1 chain, 12 double crochet into ring, slip stitch to 1st chain to join.

Round 2: * 7 chain, slip stitch into next double crochet, repeat from * to end. Fasten off.

STAR

Make 5 chains and slip stitch into 1st chain to form a ring.

Round 1: 1 chain, 18 double crochet into ring and slip stitch to 1st chain to join.

Round 2: Chain 3 (counts as 1 treble), 1 treble into each of next 2 stitches, 3 chain, * 1 treble into each of next 3 stitches, 3 chain, repeat from *to end, slip stitch to 3rd chain at beginning of round to join.

Round 3: 1 chain, 1 double crochet into next 2 stitches, (2 treble, 4 chain, 2 treble) all into next chain space, * 1 double crochet into next 3 stitches, (2 treble, 4 chain, 2 treble) all into next chain space, repeat from * to end, slip stitch to chain at beginning of round to join. Fasten off.

SPOKED MOTIF

Make 4 chains and slip stitch into 1st chain to form a ring.

Round 1: Chain 4 (counts as 1 treble and 1 chain), * 1 treble into ring, 1 chain, repeat from * 10 times more, slip stitch to 3rd chain at beginning of round. 12 spokes formed.

Round 2: Slip stitch across to 1st chain space, 3 chain, treble 2 together into same chain space (work as given for a treble until you have two loops left on your hook, work 2nd treble until 3 loops are left on your hook, wrap yarn around needle and work through all 3 loops), chain 3, * treble 3 together into next chain space (work as given for a treble until you have two loops left on your hook, work 2nd treble until 3 loops are left on your hook, work 3rd treble until 4 loops are left on your hook, wrap yarn around needle and work through all 4 loops, chain 3, repeat from * into each chain space, slip stitch to 3rd chain at beginning of round.

Round 3: Slip stitch across to next chain space, 1 chain * (2 double crochet, 4 chain, 2 double crochet) into chain space, 1 double into top of each treble 3 together of previous round, repeat from * to end, working slip stitch into chain at beginning of round instead of working a double crochet.

Fasten off.

CARTWHEEL

Make 6 chains and slip stitch into 1st chain to form a ring.

Round 1: 1 chain, 21 double crochet into ring, slip stitch to chain at beginning of round.

Round 2: 4 chain (counts as 1 treble and 1 chain), * miss 1 stitch, 1 treble into next stitch, 2 chain, repeat from * to end, slip stitch to 3rd chain at beginning of round.

Round 3: 1 chain, * 1 double crochet into next stitch, 2 double crochet into next chain space, repeat from * to end, slip stitch to chain at beginning of round. Fasten off.

MAKING UP

Lay out motifs to build a shape you like. We made ours as an smallish curved with space between motifs but you could make yours any shape or length you like remembering that a larger shape will take more yarn.

SIMPLE SHOPPING BAG
rowan handknit cotton

Materials List

YARN
Rowan Handknit Cotton
6 x 50gm
(shown in Linen 205)

HOOK
4mm (UK8/USG6) crochet hook or size
required to achieve correct tension.

FINISHED SIZE:
38cm (15¼in) wide and 42cm (16½in) deep

TENSION
16 stitches and 11 rows to 10cm (4in) measured over pattern on 4mm hook.

US crocheters please see page 44 for information about the UK/US terminology conversion.

Make 63 chains.

Round 1: 1 double crochet into 2nd chain from hook, 1 double crochet into each chain to end, 1 chain, turn work and work 1 double crochet into other side of each stitch of foundation chain row to end, slip stitch to chain at beginning of round to join. 124 stitches.

Place marker at beginning of round.

Round 2: 3 chain (counts as 1 treble), work 1 treble into each stitch to end, slip stitch to 3rd chain at beginning of round.

Round 3: 1 chain (counts as 1 double crochet), work 1 double crochet into each stitch to end, slip stitch to chain at beginning of round.

Repeat rounds 2 and 3 until work measures approx 30cm (11¾in) ending with round 2.

Work round 3 three times more, working 2 double crochet into 1 stitch on last round. 125 stitches.

Next round: 3 chain (counts as 1 treble), * skip 3 sts, work 4 trebles into next st, repeat from * to last 4 stitches, 2 treble into last stitch, slip to 3rd chain at beginning of round to join.

Next 2 rounds: As round 3.

Repeat the last 3 rounds twice more.

Next 4 rounds: As round 3. Fasten off.

HANDLES (Make 2)
Make 76 chains.

Row 1: 1 chain, 1 double crochet into each chain to end.

Repeat this row 6 times more. Fasten off.

TO MAKE UP
Sew handles to wrong side of top of bag, approx. 16cm/6¼in apart and from top of pattern band to last row to ensure they are very secure.

If you wish to make your bag a different size you will need to ensure you have a multiple of 4 stitches plus 5 in order for the pattern band to work. You may also wish to make your handles shorter or longer.

CROCHET DOTS NECKLACE
rowan pure linen or handknit cotton

Materials List

YARN
Rowan Pure Linen
1 x 50gm
(shown in Atacama 392)
Rowan Handknit Cotton
1 x 50gm
(shown in Delphinium 334 and Ochre 349)

HOOKS
1 3mm (UK 11/US C2/D3) crochet hook for Rowan Pure Linen
1 3.5mm (UK 9/US E4 crochet hook for Rowan Handknit Cotton

TENSION:

Tension is not essential for this project as there is no set length as you will work to the length desired.

US crocheters please see page 44 for information about the UK/US terminology conversion.

We made our necklaces 114cm (45in) and 70cm (27in) in length

The basis of our necklace is a long thread of chains with large and small dots worked at random along its length before being joined to the start of the thread with a slip stitch to form a ring. You will need to work a few chains before working the first dot and you will also need to work a few chains between each dot to stop them gathering up too much.

The idea is for you to play and create your own necklace style.

LARGE DOTS

Work 3 chains, slip stitch to first of these chains to create a ring. Work 3 chains, turn and work 14 trebles into this ring, slip stitch to join to 3rd chain at beginning of round working through the 2nd chain along your necklace thread.

SMALL DOTS

Work 3 chains, slip stitch to first of these chains to create a ring. Work 1 chain, turn and work 9 double crochet into this ring, slip stitch to join to chain at beginning of round working through the 1st chain along your necklace thread.

GRANNY SQUARE CUSHION
rowan creative focus worsted

Materials List

YARN
Rowan Creative Focus Worsted
2 [3] x 100gm
(16 in cushion size shown in Charcoal
Heather 00402)

HOOK
5mm (UK6/USH8) crochet hook or size
required to achieve correct square
size.

Finished size - approx 41cm (16in) or 46cm (18in) square

TENSION
Trebles should be 1.5cm in height worked on 5mm hook.

US crocheters please see page 44 for information about the UK/US terminology conversion.

LARGER SQUARE (MAKE 1)
Using 5mm crochet hook make 4 chains, slip stitch into 1st chain to form a ring.

Round 1: 3 chain (counts as 1 treble), 2 treble, (2 chain, 3 treble) 3 times, 2 chain, slip stitch into 3rd chain at beginning of round to join, turn.

Round 2: 3 chain (counts as 1 treble), (2 treble, 2 chain, 3 treble) all into same chain space, * 2 chain, 3 treble, 2 chain, 3 treble) into next chain space, repeat from * twice more, 2 chain, using colour B slip stitch to 3rd chain at beginning of round, turn.

Round 3: 3 chain (counts as 1 treble), 2 treble into same chain space, * 2 chain, (3 treble, 2 chain, 3 treble) into corner chain space, 2 chain, 3 treble into next chain space, repeat from * twice more, 2 chain, (3 treble, 2 chain, 3 treble) into corner chain space,

slip stitch to 3rd chain at beginning of round, turn.

Round 4: 3 chain (counts as 1 treble), 2 treble into same chain space, * 2 chain, (3 treble, 2 chain, 3 treble) into corner chain space, (2 chain, 3 treble into next chain space) twice, repeat from * twice more, 2 chain, (3 treble, 2 chain, 3 treble) into corner chain space, 2 chain, 3 treble into next chain space, 2 chain, slip stitch to 3rd chain at beginning of round, turn.

Round 5: 3 chain (counts as 1 treble), 2 treble into same chain space, 2 chain, 3 treble into next chain space, * 2 chain, (3 treble, 2 chain, 3 treble) into corner chain space, (2 chain, 3 treble into next chain space) 3 times, repeat from * twice more, 2 chain, (3 treble, 2 chain, 3 treble) into corner chain space, 2 chain, 3 treble into next chain space, 2 chain, slip stitch to 3rd chain at beginning of round.

Round 5 sets pattern, continue in this way working an extra 2 chain, 3 treble into next chain space on each side on every further round.

Continue in this way until you have worked 14 [18] rounds.
(Work should now meas 41 [46] cm/16 [18]in)

Fasten off.

SMALLER SQUARES (MAKE 4)

Work as given for Larger square for
7 [9] rounds.

Fasten off.

Sew in all ends and press lightly.

MAKING UP

Join the four smaller squares to form
a larger square. You can choose to
slip stitch crochet or sew together.
We stitched ours together using the
outer loops of the last round.

Join the two squares around three
edges, insert cushion pad before
joining fourth side seam. We used a
brightly coloured cushion inside to
create a contrast effect.

GRANNY SQUARE BLANKET
rowan pure wool superwash worsted

Materials List

YARN
Rowan Pure Wool Superwash Worsted
A – Mustard 131   3 x 100gm
B – Granite 111   14 x 100gm

HOOK
5mm (UK6/USH8) crochet hook or size required to achieve correct square size.

FINISHED SIZE:
approx – 154cm (60½in) x
182cm (71½in)

TENSION
Each square should measure
approx 15cm (6in)

**US crocheters please see page
44 for information about the UK/US
terminology conversion.**

Using 5mm crochet hook and A
make 4 chains, slip stitch into 1st
chain to form a ring.

Round 1: 3 chain (counts as 1
treble), 2 treble, (2 chain, 3 treble)
3 times into ring, 2 chain, slip stitch
into 3rd chain at beginning of round
to join, turn.

Round 2: 3 chain (counts as 1
treble), (2 treble, 2 chain, 3 treble)
all into same chain space, * 2
chain, (3 treble, 2 chain, 3 treble)
into next chain space, repeat
from * twice more, 2 chain, using
colour B slip stitch to 3rd chain at
beginning of round, turn.

Continue using colour
B throughout.

Round 3: 3 chain (counts as 1
treble), 2 treble into same chain
space, * 2 chain, (3 treble, 2 chain,
3 treble) into corner chain space,
2 chain, 3 treble into next chain
space, repeat from * twice more,

2 chain, (3 treble, 2 chain, 3 treble)
into corner chain space, 3 chain,
slip stitch to 3rd chain at beginning
of round, turn.

Round 4: 3 chain (counts as 1
treble), 2 treble into same chain
space, * 2 chain, (3 treble, 2
chain, 3 treble) into corner chain
space, (2 chain, 3 treble into next
chain space) twice, repeat from
* twice more, 2 chain, (3 treble, 2
chain, 3 treble) into corner chain
space, 2 chain, 3 treble into next
chain space, 2 chain, slip stitch
to 3rd chain at beginning of
round, turn.

Round 5: 3 chain (counts as 1
treble), 2 treble into same chain
space, 2 chain, 3 treble into next
chain space, * 2 chain, (3 treble, 2
chain, 3 treble) into corner chain
space, (2 chain, 3 treble into next
chain space) 3 times, repeat from
* twice more, 2 chain, (3 treble, 2
chain, 3 treble) into corner chain
space, 2 chain, 3 treble into next
chain space, 2 chain, slip stitch
to 3rd chain at beginning of
round, turn.

Round 6: 3 chain (counts as 1
treble), 2 treble into same chain
space, 2 chain, 3 treble into next
chain space, * 2 chain, (3 treble, 2
chain, 3 treble) into corner chain
space, (2 chain, 3 treble into next
chain space) 4 times, repeat from
* twice more, 2 chain, (3 treble, 2
chain, 3 treble) into corner chain
space, (2 chain, 3 treble into next
chain space) twice,

2 chain, slip stitch to 3rd chain at beginning of round.

Fasten off.

Sew in all ends and press lightly.

Make a further 98 squares in the same way.

MAKING UP

Join all squares, making your final blanket 9 squares wide and 11 squares deep. You can choose to slip stitch crochet or sew together. We used slip stitch crochet to give a raised seam.

DOILY BUNTING
rowan handknit cotton

Materials List

YARN
Rowan Handknit Cotton
Each 50gm ball of yarn will make
31/2 motifs.
We used Sea Foam 352, Celery 309
and Delphinium 334

HOOK
5mm (UK6/USH8) crochet hook or size
required to achieve correct tension.

TENSION

Trebles should be 1.5cm in height worked on 5mm hook.

US crocheters please see page 44 for information about the UK/US terminology conversion.

Make 7 chains and slip stitch into 1st chain to form a ring.

Round 1: Chain 3 (counts as 1 treble), treble 2 together into ring (work as given for a treble until you have two loops left on your hook, work 2nd treble until 3 loops are left on your hook, wrap yarn around needle and work through all 3 loops), chain 3, * treble 3 together into ring (work as given for a treble until you have two loops left on your hook, work 2nd treble until 3 loops are left on your hook, work 3rd treble until 4 loops are left on your hook, wrap yarn around needle and work through all 4 loops, chain 3, rep from * 7 times more, join with 1 treble into top of first cluster/spoke. (9 spokes formed)

Round 2: Chain 3 (counts as 1 treble), treble 2 together into chain space just formed by trebling into cluster, * 5 chain, treble 3 together into next chain space, repeat from * to 7 times more, treble 3 together into next chain space, 1 chain, join with 1 treble into top of first cluster/spoke.

Round 3: Chain 3 (counts as 1 treble), treble 2 together into chain space just formed by trebling into cluster, chain 3, treble 3 together into same chain space * 3 chain, treble 3 together, chain 3, treble 3 together into next chain space, repeat from * 7 times more, join with 1 treble into top of first cluster/spoke.

Round 4: Chain 1, 5 treble into chain space just formed by trebling into cluster, slip stitch into top of next cluster/spoke , 3 treble into next chain space, slip stitch into top of next cluster/spoke, * 5 treble into next chain space, slip stitch into top of next cluster/spoke, 3 treble into next chain space, slip stitch into next cluster/spoke, repeat from * to end, ending last repeat with slip stitch to top of first cluster.

Fasten off.

If you wish to make a larger doily repeat round 3 until doily is desired size.

ENVELOPE CUSHION
rowan pure wool worsted

Materials List

YARN
Rowan Pure Wool Worsted
4 [4] x 100gm
(shown in Toffee 104 and
Moonstone 112)
With oddments of Kidsilk Haze in
Majestic 589 or Trance 582 and Jelly
597 for embellishment.

HOOK
5mm (UK6/USH8) crochet hook or
size required to achieve correct
square size.
4mm (UK8/USG6) crochet hook for
embellishment.

FINISHED SIZE
approx – 41cm (16in) or 46cm (18in) square

TENSION
18 stitches and 11 rows to 10cm (4in) measured over pattern on 5mm(UK6/USH8) hook.

US crocheters please see page 44 for information about the UK/US terminology conversion.

Make 75 [84] chains.

Foundation row (Right Side): Miss 1st chain, 1 double crochet into each chain to end, turn. 74 [83] stitches.

Row 2: Chain 3 (counts as 1st treble), miss 1st stitch, working through front loop (the one nearest you only) work 1 treble into each stitch to end, work 1 treble into chain at beginning of last row, turn.

Row 3: Chain 3 (counts as 1st treble), miss 1st stitch, working through back loop only (the one furthest away from you) work 1 treble into each stitch to end, work 1 treble into 3rd chain at beginning of last row, turn.

Row 4: Chain 1 (counts as 1st double crochet), miss 1st stitch, working through front loop only work 1 double crochet into each stitch to end, work 1 double crochet into 3rd chain at beginning of last row.

Row 5: Chain 1 (counts as 1st double crochet), miss 1st stitch, working through back loop only work 1 double crochet into each stitch to end, work 1 double crochet into chain at beginning of last row, turn.

Rows 2 to 5 set pattern.

Working in pattern as set throughout continue until work measures 82 [92]cm/32¼ [36¼]in.

Place a marker at end of last row.

Cont in pattern until work measures approx. 16 [18]cm/6¼[7]in from marker, ending with row 3 of pattern.

Next row: 1 chain (counts as 1 double crochet), miss 1st stitch, 1 double crochet into each stitch to end, work 1 double crochet into 3rd chain and beginning of last row.

FASTENING STRAP
Make 77 [86] chains.

Foundation row (Right Side): Miss 1st chain, 1 double crochet into each chain to end, turn. 76 [85] stitches.

Row 1: 1 chain (counts as 1 double crochet), miss 1st stitch, 1 double crochet into each stitch to end, work 1 double crochet into 3rd chain and beginning of last row, turn.

Rows 2 to 6: Work as given for row 1.

Fasten off.

MAKING UP

Place fastening strap approx 10 [12] cm/4 [4¾]in down from foundation row on right side of fabric and pin in place.

With right sides of fabric facing inwards fold cushion in half so that the foundation row meets the marker. You can now join the side seams trapping the fastening strap in position.

You may wish to add dots of colour to your cushions as shown in the photograph.

LARGE DOTS

Using 4mm hook and two ends of Kidsilk Haze held together make 4 chains, slip stitch into 1st chain to form a ring.

Round 1: 3 chain, 11 treble into ring, slip stitch to 3rd chain at beginning of round to join. 12 stitches.

Round 2: 3 chain, * 2 treble into next stitch, 1 treble into next stitch, repeat from * to end, slip stitch to 3rd chain at beginning of round to join. 18 stitches.

Round 3: 3 chain, * 2 treble into next stitch, 1 treble into next 2 stitches,

repeat from * to end, slip stitch to 3rd chain at beginning of round to join. 24 stitches.

Round 4: 3 chain, * 2 treble into next stitch, 1 treble into next 3 stitches, repeat from * to end, slip stitch to 3rd chain at beginning of round to join. 30 stitches.

Round 5: 3 chain, * 2 treble into next stitch, 1 treble into next 4 stitches, repeat from * to end, slip stitch to 3rd chain at beginning of round to join. 36 stitches.

Fasten off.

MEDIUM DOT

Work as given for large dot until round 4 has been completed. Fasten off.

SMALL DOT

Work as given for large dot until round 2 has been completed. Fasten off.

SHELL STITCH BED RUNNER
rowan creative focus worsted

Materials List

YARN
Rowan Creative Focus Worsted
11 x 100gm
(shown in Blue Smoke 03089)

HOOK
5.5mm (UK5/USI9) crochet hook or size
required to achieve correct tension.

FINISHED SIZE:
approx – 90cm (35½in) wide x
200cm (78¾in) in length

**US crocheters please see page
44 for information about the UK/US
terminology conversion.**

TENSION
2 pattern repeats measures 10cm
(4in) wide and 3cm (1¼in) deep.

Using 5.5mm crochet hook and A
make 111 chains. (or a multiple of
6 plus 3 to desired width)

Row 1: 1 chain, 1 double crochet
into each chain to end.

Row 2: 1 chain, 1 double crochet
into each stitch to end.

Row 3: 3 chain, * (2 treble, 1 chain,
2 treble) into next stitch, miss 2
stitches, (1 treble, 1 chain, 1 treble)
into next stitch, miss 2 stitches,
repeat from * to end, ending row
with (2 treble, 1 chain, 2 treble) into
1 stitch, 1 treble into last stitch.

Row 4: 3 chain, * (2 treble, 1 chain,
2 treble) into next chain space,
miss 3 stitches, (1 treble, 1 chain, 1
treble) into next chain space, miss
3 stitches, repeat from * to end,

ending row with (2 treble, 1 chain,
2 treble into 1 stitch), 1 treble into
last stitch.

Row 4 sets pattern.

Continue as set until work
measures 199cm (78¼in).

Work as set on row 2, twice more.

Fasten off.

If you wish to amend the size of
your blanket you will need to
make sure when you make your
foundation chains you have a
multiple of 6 plus 3 chains in order
for the pattern to work correctly.

Information

UK vs US crochet abbreviations

In this book we have used UK crochet terms which differ slightly to the US terms. Whilst In this book we have given you a description of how each stitch is worked, we have included a couple of UK terms and the relative US terms for your future reference.

UK	US
Double crochet	**Single crochet**
Treble	**Double crochet**

Tension

This is the size of your crochet. Most of the patterns will have a tension quoted. This is how many stitches in width and how many rows in length It takes to make a 10cm/4in square. If your crochet doesn't match this then your finished garment will not measure the correct size. To obtain the correct measurements for your garment you must achieve the tension.

The tension quoted on a ball band is the manufacturer's average. For the manufacturer and designers to produce designs they have to use a tension for you to be able to obtain the measurements quoted. It's fine not to be the average, but you need to know if you meet the average or not. Then you can make the necessary adjustments to obtain the correct measurements.

How to make a Tension Square

First of all look at the tension details in your pattern. For example it might say "20 stitches and 28 rows to 10cm/4in measured over pattern using a 4mm crochet hook". Make sure you use the correct yarn and needles. Make your initial chain at least 4 extra stitches than the tension states (this will give you the true width of all stitches) and work at least 4 extra rows.

Your work might be looser or tighter than the tension required, in which case you just need to alter your hook size. Go up one size if you have an extra stitch or two sizes if you have two extra stitches and the reverse if you have fewer stitches.

Choosing Yarn

Choosing yarn, as one of my friends once described "It is like shopping in an adult's sweetie shop". I think this sums it up very well. All the colours and textures, where do you start? Look for the thickness,

how chunky do you want your finished garment? Sometimes it's colour that draws you to a yarn or perhaps you have a pattern that requires a specific yarn. Check the washing/care instructions before you buy.

Yarn varies in thickness; there are various descriptions such as DK and 4ply these are examples of standard weights. There are a lot of yarns available that are not standard and it helps to read the ball band to see what the recommended hook size is. This will give you an idea of the approximate thickness. It is best to use the yarn recommended in the pattern.

Keep one ball band from each project so that you have a record of what you have used and most importantly how to care for your garment after it has been completed. Always remember to give the ball band with the garment if it is a gift.

The ball band normally provides you with the average tension and recommended hook sizes for the yarn, this may vary from what has been used in the pattern, always go with the pattern as the designer may change needles to obtain a certain look. The ball band also tells you the name of the yarn and what it is made of, the weight and approximate length of the ball of yarn along with the shade and dye lot numbers. This is important as dye lots can vary, you need to buy your yarn with matching dye lots.

YARN AMOUNTS ARE BASED ON AVERAGE REQUIREMENT AND ARE THEREFORE APPROXIMATE

Pressing and Aftercare.

Having spent so long knitting your project it can be a great shame not to look after it properly. Some yarns are suitable for pressing once you have finished to improve the look of the fabric. To find out this information you will need to look on the yarn ball band, where there will be washing and care symbols.

Once you have checked to see if your yarn is suitable to be pressed and the knitting is a smooth texture (stocking stitch for example), pin out and place a damp cloth onto the knitted pieces. Hold the steam iron (at the correct temperature) approximately 10cm/4in away from the fabric and steam. Keep the knitted pieces pinned in place until cool.

As a test it is a good idea to wash your tension square in the way you would expect to wash your garment.

Stockists

AUSTRALIA: Australian Country Spinners, Pty Ltd, Level 7, 409 St. Kilda Road,Melbourne Vic 3004. Tel: 03 9380 3888 Fax: 03 9820 0989 Email: customerservice@auspinners.com.au

AUSTRIA: Coats Harlander Ges.m.b.H.., Autokaderstraße 29, 1210 Wien, Austria Tel: 00800 26 27 28 00 Fax: (00) 49 7644 802-133 Email: coats.harlander@coats.com Web: www.coatscrafts.at

BELGIUM: Coats N.V., c/o Coats GmbH Kaiserstr.1 79341 Kenzingen Germany Tel: 0032 (0) 800 77 89 2 Fax: 00 49 7644 802 133 Email: sales.coatsninove@coats.com Web: www.coatscrafts.be

BULGARIA: Coats Bulgaria, 7 Magnaurska Shkola Str., BG-1784 Sofia, Bulgaria Tel: (+359 2) 976 77 41 Fax: (+359 2) 976 77 20 Email: officebg@coats.com Web: www.coatsbulgaria.bg

CANADA: Westminster Fibers, 10 Roybridge Gate, Suite 200, Vaughan, Ontario L4H 3M8 Tel: (800) 263-2354 Fax: 905-856-6184 Email: info@westminsterfibers.com

CHINA: Coats Shanghai Ltd, No 9 Building , Baosheng Road, Songjiang Industrial Zone, Shanghai. Tel: (86- 21) 13816681825 Fax: (86-21) 57743733-326 Email: victor.li@coats.com

CYPRUS: Coats Bulgaria, 7 Magnaurska Shkola Str., BG-1784 Sofia, Bulgaria Tel: (+359 2) 976 77 41 Fax: (+359 2) 976 77 20 Email: officebg@coats.com Web: www.coatscrafts.com.cy

CZECH REPUBLIC: Coats Czecho s.r.o.Staré Mesto 246 569 32Tel: (420) 461616633 Email: galanterie@coats.com

ESTONIA: Coats Eesti AS, Ampri tee 9/4, 74001 Viimsi HarjumaaTel: +372 630 6250 Fax: +372 630 6260 Email: info@coats.ee Web: www.coatscrafts.co.ee

DENMARK: Carl J. Permin A/S Egegaardsvej 28 DK-2610 Rødovre Tel: (45) 36 72 12 00 E-mail: permin@permin.dk

FINLAND: Coats Opti Crafts Oy, Huhtimontie 6 04200 KERAVA Tel: (358) 9 274871 Email: coatsopti.sales@coats.com www.coatscrafts.fi

FRANCE: Coats France, c/o Coats GmbH, Kaiserstr.1, 79341 Kenzingen, Germany Tel: (0) 0810 06 00 02 Email: artsdufil@coats.com Web: www.coatscrafts.fr

GERMANY: Coats GmbH, Kaiserstr. 1, 79341 Kenzingen, Germany Tel: 0049 7644 802 222 Email: kenzingen.vertrieb@coats.com Fax: 0049 7644 802 30 Web: www.coatsgmbh.de

GREECE: Coats Bulgaria, 7 Magnaurska Shkola Str., BG-1784 Sofia, Bulgaria Tel: (+359 2) 976 77 41 Fax: (+359 2) 976 77 20 Email: officebg@coats.com Web: www.coatscrafts.gr

HOLLAND: Coats B.V., c/o Coats GmbH, Kaiserstr.1, 79341 Kenzingen, Germany Tel: 0031 (0) 800 02 26 6488 Fax: 00 49 7644 802 133 Email: sales.coatsninove@coats.com Web: www.coatscrafts.be

HONG KONG: East Unity Company Ltd, Unit B2, 7/F., Block B, Kailey Industrial Centre, 12 Fung Yip Street, Chai Wan Tel: (852)2869 7110 Email: eastunityco@yahoo.com.hk

ICELAND: Storkurinn, Laugavegi 59, 101 Reykjavik Tel: (354) 551 8258 Email: storkurinn@simnet.is

ITALY: Coats Cucirini srl, Viale Sarca no 223, 20126 Milano Tel: 02636151 Fax: 0266111701

KOREA: Coats Korea Co. Ltd, 5F Eyeon B/D, 935-40 Bangbae-Dong, 137-060 Tel: (82) 2 521 6262 Fax: (82) 2 521 5181 Email: rozenpark@coats.com

LATVIA: Coats Latvija SIA, Mukusalas str. 41 b, Riga LV-1004 Tel: +371 67 625173 Fax: +371 67 892758 Email: info.latvia@coats.com Web: www.coatscrafts.lv

LEBANON: y.knot, Saifi Village, Mkhalissiya Street 162, BeirutTel: (961) 1 992211 Fax: (961) 1 315553 Email: y.knot@cyberia.net.lb

LITHUANIA & RUSSIA: Coats Lietuva UAB, A. Juozapaviciaus str. 6/2, LT-09310 Vilnius Tel: +370 527 30971 Fax: +370 527 2305 Email: info@coats.lt Web: www.coatscrafts.lt

LUXEMBOURG: Coats N.V., c/o Coats GmbH, Kaiserstr.1, 79341 Kenzingen, Germany Tel: 00 49 7644 802 222 Fax: 00 49 7644 802 133 Email: sales.coatsninove@coats.com Web: www.coatscrafts.be

MALTA: John Gregory Ltd, 8 Ta'Xbiex Sea Front, Msida MSD 1512, Malta Tel: +356 2133 0202 Fax: +356 2134 4745 Email: raygreg@onvol.net

MEXICO: Estambres Crochet SA de CV, Aaron Saenz 1891-7, PO Box SANTAMARIA, 64650 MONTERREY TEL +52 (81) 8335-3870

NEW ZEALAND: ACS New Zealand, P.O Box 76199, Northwood, Christchurch New Zealand Tel: 64 3 323 6665 Fax: 64 3 323 6660 Email: lynn@impactmg.co.nz

NORWAY: Falk Knappehuset AS, Svinesundsveien 347, 1788 Halden, Norway Tel: +47 555 393 00 Email: post@falkgruppen.no

PORTUGAL: Coats & Clark, Quinta de Cravel, Apartado 444, 4431-968 Portugal Tel: 00 351 223 770700

SINGAPORE: Golden Dragon Store, 101 Upper Cross Street #02-51, People's Park Centre, Singapore 058357 Tel: (65) 6 5358454 Fax: (65) 6 2216278 Email: gdscraft@hotmail.com

SLOVAKIA: Coats s.r.o.Kopcianska 94851 01 Bratislava Tel: (421) 263532314 Email: galanteria@coats.com

SOUTH AFRICA: Arthur Bales LTD, 62 4th Avenue, Linden 2195 Tel: (27) 11 888 2401 Fax: (27) 11 782 6137 Email: arthurb@new.co.za

SPAIN: Coats Fabra SAU, Avda Meridiana 350, pta 13, 08027 Barcelona Tel: (34) 932908400 Fax: 932908409 Email: atencion.clientes@coats.com

SWEDEN: Bröderna Falk Sybehör & Garn Engros, Stationsvägen 2, 516 31 Dalsjöfors Tel: (46) 40-6084002 Fax: 033-7207940 Email: kundtjanst@falk.se

SWITZERLAND: Coats Stroppel AG, Stroppelstrasse 20, 5417 Untersiggenthal, Switzerland Tel: 00800 2627 2800 Fax: 0049 7644 802 133 Email: coats.stroppel@coats.com Web: www.coatscrafts.ch

TAIWAN: Cactus Quality Co Ltd, 7FL-2, No. 140, Sec.2 Roosevelt Rd, Taipei, 10084 Taiwan, R.O.C. Tel: 00886-2-23656527 Fax: 886-2-23656503 Email: cqcl@ms17.hinet.net

THAILAND: Global Wide Trading, 10 Lad Prao Soi 88, Bangkok 10310 Tel: 00 662 933 9019 Fax: 00 662 933 9110 Email: global.wide@yahoo.com

U.S.A.: Westminster Fibers, 8 Shelter Drive, Greer, South Carolina, 29650 Tel: (800) 445-9276 Fax: 864-879-9432 Email: info@westminsterfibers.com

U.K: Rowan, Green Lane Mill, Holmfirth, West Yorkshire, England HD9 2DX Tel: +44 (0) 1484 681881 Fax: +44 (0) 1484 687920 Email: ccuk.sales@coats.com Web: www.knitrowan.com

Credits

Thanks to:-

James Green - Printworks on Folksy
www.folksy.com/shops/
jamesgreenprintworks

Grey Suit clay
www.greysuitclay.com

Roanna Wells
www.roannawells.co.uk

Peggypeg
www.folksy.com/shops/peggy

Acknowledgements

Many thanks to everyone who made this book possible. From my amazing team of knitters to India for being a joy to work with and making the projects look stunning.

A special thanks also to Kate Buller and the team at Rowan for all their continued support.